THE EAGLE
IN THE EULACHON

Written by

Linda Buckley

Illustrated by

Robin K. Robbins

The Eagle in the Eulachon

A children's book on deep ecology

Text: Linda Buckley
Illustrations: Robin K. Robbins
Eagle consultant: Chris Niemela
Layout and Design: Mary Meade
Copyright@2024 Linda Buckley

Eagle and eagle feather drawings pgs 40, 42–45:
Elias Buckley (Grandson of the author)
Designed in the USA

Alaskasong, Inc. Publisher
Juneau, Alaska
lindagramma@gmail.com

Dedicated to my daughter, Cadie.

Like eagles, she opens her wings to

the next adventure and flies!

THE EAGLE IN THE EULACHON

EULACHON

Eulachon pronounced "hooligan" are slender,
silvery fish with a bluish back and a white
belly. They are sometimes called "candlefish"
because their oily flesh burns like a candle
when dried.

Can you see the eagle in the eulachon (hooligan)?

No.

Can you see the sun in the eulachon?

Yes.

Can you see the rain in the eulachon?

Yes.

Can you see the ocean in the eulachon?

Yes.

When the eulachon return to rivers to lay their eggs,
it causes a feeding frenzy.

How do eagles see fish underwater?

Eagles have special eyes so they can see fish underwater.

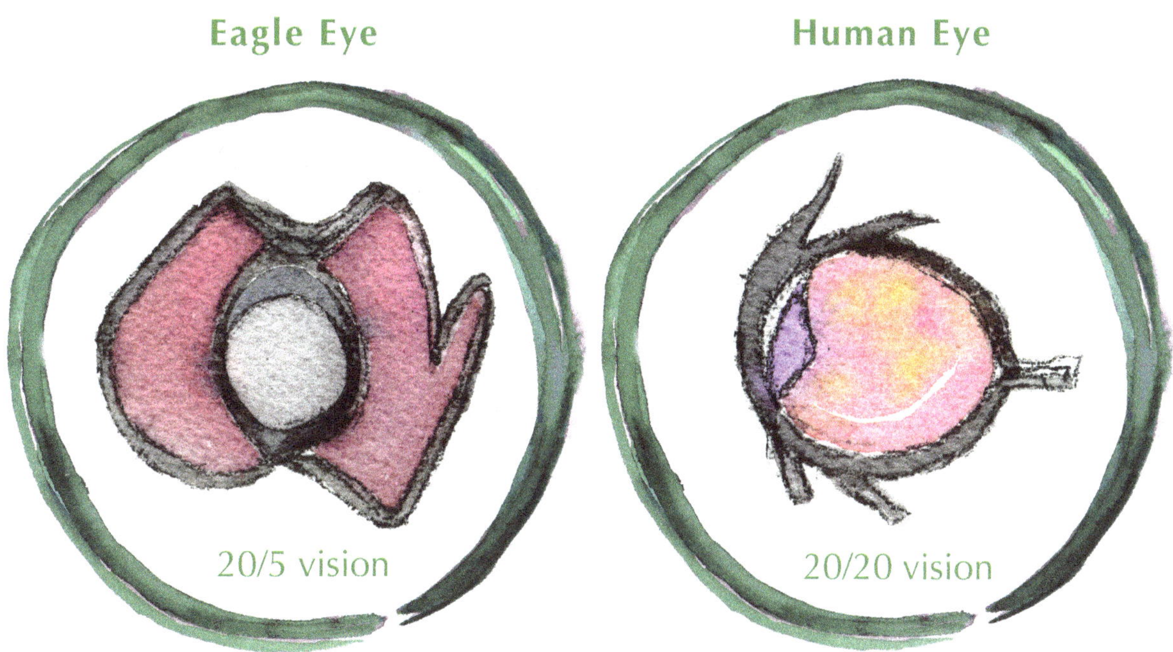

They can see two miles (3.2 kilometers) away.

What happens after the eagle eats a lot of eulachon?

The eagle has to go poop!

Sometimes they poop while they're flying.
Look out below!

When the eagle poops in the water, eulachon and other fish swim through the poopy water. The eulachon absorb the nutrients from the eagle poop!

Eagles mate for life. When eagles find a mate,
they do a cartwheel dance in the air.

They fly high into the sky and lock their talons.

They tumble, and spin together letting go
right before they hit the ground.

Once they find a mate, they look for a tall tree to build their nest. They use the same nest every year.

The female will lay one or two eggs. Both parents take turns sitting on the eggs for 35 days.

After the eggs hatch, both parents bring
food to the new eaglets.

The babies are hungry and keep their parents
busy catching fish.

When the baby eagles grow bigger, they will grab the food from their parents and feed themselves.

Twelve weeks after they hatch, the baby
eagles are ready to fly.

They practice flapping their wings.

Even after the young eagles learn to fly, the parents
bring them larger and larger fish.

Then they teach them how to catch their own.

If the eagle drops a fish in the water, she will have
to swim after it.

Then the eagle has to dry her wings before
she can fly again.

Adult bald eagles have a white head and tail.

Young eagles start out all one color. It takes almost five years for them to have a white head and tail.

During those five years, the juvenile eagles appear
larger than their parents.

The cycle repeats year after year.

Find a mate, build a nest, lay some eggs,
feed the young, and fly away.

Every spring the eulachon return.

Now do you see the eagle in the eulachon?

Keep looking.

Remember the eagle poop?

Where did the eagle poop go?

The poop landed in the ocean
and the eulachon swam through it.

Everything is in the eulachon.

The sun, the rain, the ocean and the eagle.

It's the circle of life.

THE END

NOW,

follow the feathers

and learn some "eagle facts"

that might surprise you."

!

EAGLE FACTS:

How fast can eagles fly?

Eagles can fly up to 30 miles per hour.

How fast are they going when they dive to catch a fish?

They can dive up to 100 miles per hour. They have to be fast or the fish will swim away.

How long can an eagle live in the wild?

An eagle can live to be 30 years old in the wild.

How big is an eagle's nest?

An eagle nest reaches 9 feet in diameter and can weigh 2000 pounds!

How high up in the sky can an eagle fly?

An eagle can reach altitudes of over 10,000 feet.

Why are they called "bald" eagles when they're not bald?

Their name comes from an old English word, "piebald" which means white-headed.

What is the wingspan of an adult eagle?

An eagle wingspan can go from five and a half feet to eight feet.

How do eagles avoid the rain?

They fly above the clouds.

What do eagles eat besides fish?

They will eat seabirds, ducks and small mammals such as rabbits or squirrels. But their favorite food is fish.

Do eagles molt?

Yes. Every year their old feathers fall out and new ones replace them.

Is it legal to collect eagle feathers?

Only if you are a Native American. Eagles are protected by Federal Law. If you are caught with any part of an eagle you could go to prison for one year and/or pay a $5000 fine.

What is one impact of climate change on bald eagles?

As the ocean temperatures rise, the salmon are threatened. This is the eagle's main food source.

Do humans eat eulachon?

Yes. They dip nets to scoop up the fish. They can smoke, dry, can and freeze them.

Where do the eulachon spawn in Alaska?

Along the dark area on the map.

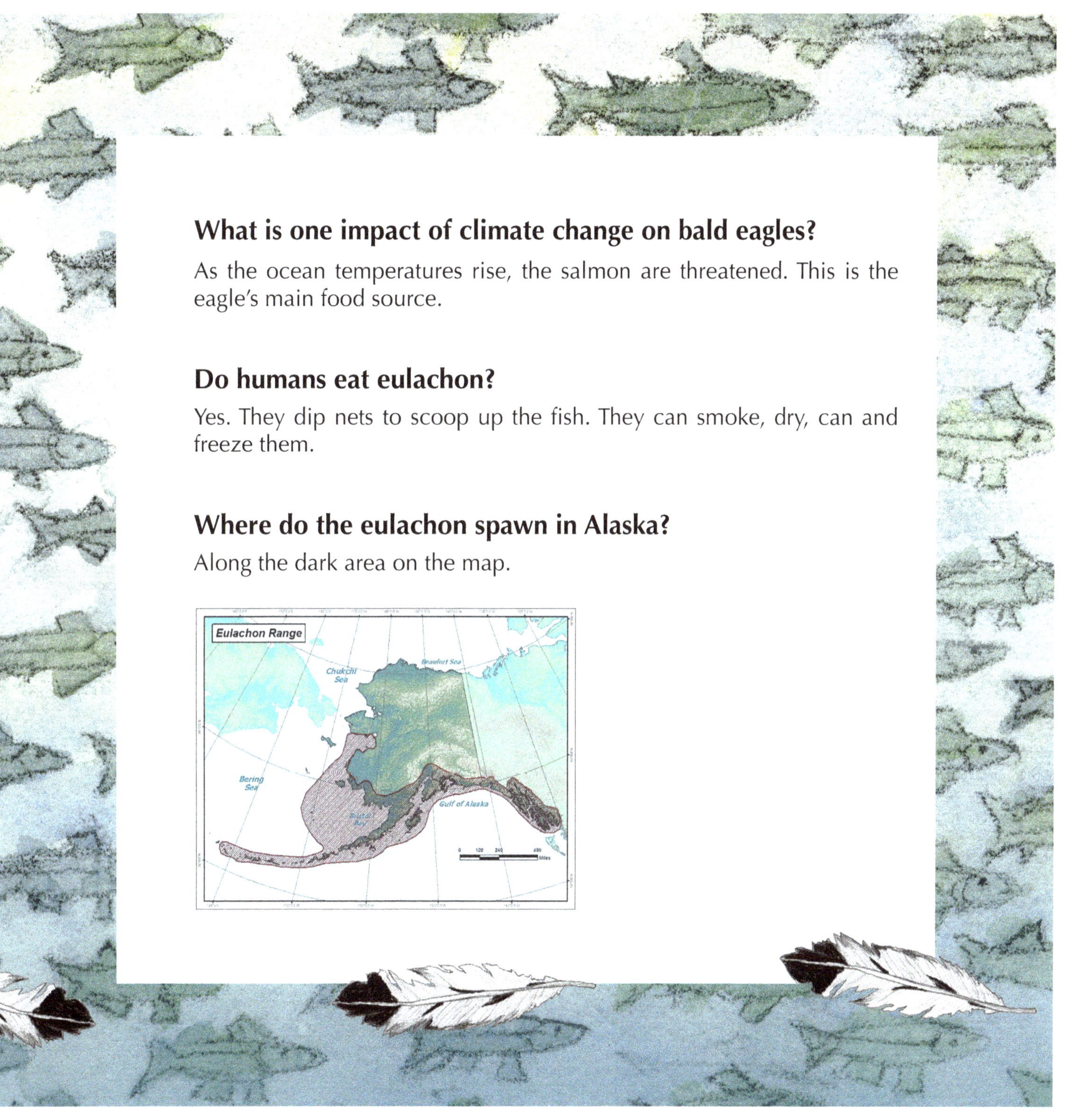

About the Author

Linda Buckley has lived in Alaska for over 50 years. She taught music, art, outdoor education, and Alaska culture classes. She also served as the librarian in a small rural school in Southeast Alaska. Her songs have been recorded on four CD's. She published her first children's book, *The Bear in the Blueberry* in 2019. She published *The Humpback in the Herring* in 2021 and her first collection of poetry, *Made of Rain* in 2022. *The Eagle in the Eulachon* is the third in a series about the interconnectedness of all things. Linda is an active environmentalist and hopes that these books will inspire young people to care for the earth as they understand how everything is connected to everything.

About the Illustrator

Robin Kinney Robbins lives in Seattle, Washington. Robin taught in the Peace Corps and in Washington Public Schools for 38 years. She taught art alongside bilingual education. Robin travels with her paints, not with a camera. She has painted in Peru, Ecuador, Mexico, Cambodia, Vietnam, Laos, and Europe. She has exhibited her work in galleries in Seattle and in her second home in Chautauqua, New York. She illustrated her first book, *The Bear in the Blueberry* in 2019 and her second book, *The Humpback in the Herring* in 2021. *The Eagle in the Eulachon* is her third children's book.